If God Used Sticky Notes®

From: God
To: All

Keep these
in your heart!
love,
God

Chris Shea

HARVEST HOUSE PUBLISHERS

EUGENE, OREGON

Cover by Garborg Design Works, Savage, Minnesota
If God Used Sticky Notes® is a Registered Trademark of Chris Shea

If God Used Sticky Notes ®

Copyright © 2007 by Chris Shea
Lifesighs Cards, PO Box 19446, San Diego, CA 92159

Published by Harvest House Publishers
Eugene, Oregon 97402
www.harvesthousepublishers.com

ISBN-13: 978-0-7369-1852-7

Printed in China
11 12 13 14 15 / LP / 11 10 9 8 7 6

For my friend Corinne.
Surely a gift sent to me from God.

CS

Where would you most like
to see one and what
would you like it to say

4

If God set out
a few sticky notes

along your pathway today?

Maybe on the mirror
in the bathroom

Good morning!
I'll be with you
all day. Just pray
if you need anything.
love, God
This is the day which the
Lord hath made.
- Ps. 118:24

or on the morning newspaper's front page

Don't let the news
get you down!
love,
God
Peace be within thee.
Ps. 122:8
DAILY NEWS
BIG STORM

on the razor we shave with

Anything you have to face, I'll be there too. You _were_ made in my reflection, after all... love, God
Arise, shine; for thy light is come.
                                                    -Is. 60:1

the toothbrush we brush with

14

Speak kind
words today!
love,
God

Then the Lord put forth
his hand and touched
my mouth. Jer. 1:9

on the carton of milk

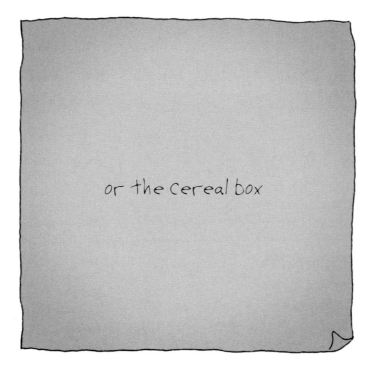

or the cereal box

or our umbrellas
beside the front door.

20

Take your childlike enthusiasm with you today! Look for good puddles!
love, God

Thou visitest the earth and waterest it.
Ps. 65:9

What if we found them
all day long-
little colored squares
of paper stuck
on everything

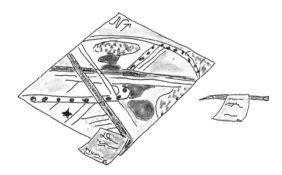

reminding us of God's constancy

his compassion and his care?

A pink one on the doorknob
as we head out
for the day

26

Remember...
There's nothing you
can't do with your
hand in mine!
love, God

I will go in the strength
of the Lord.
Ps. 71:16

27

a blue one on a magazine
in the doctor's
waiting room

a yellow one on a taxi door
as we head out on a trip

or a lavender one
on the nightstand
to read before we sleep.

Of course, if we really think about it

God's sticky notes are all around

because his messages
of goodness

36

always find their way

through sight

or sound

39

or fragrance

soft

or touch

into everyone's
expectant heart

where they stick secure, forever.

A bird

ω   ω   ω

in flight

45

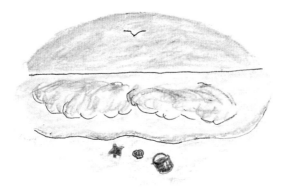

the ocean as it greets the shore

snow floating down from above

the beautiful sight

of a face we love

the sound of a voice we miss

the feel of a hand we love to hold

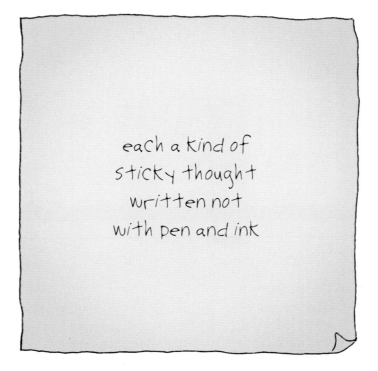

each a kind of
sticky thought
written not
with pen and ink

52

but written nonetheless
for every heart
to keep.

Where would I like to see one

and what would I like it to say

if God put a little sticky note
along your path today?

I'd like him to put it on a star

somewhere beyond the moon

and I'd like it to say

as only God could

This is
how far my love for
you goes... to the
moon and back
forever! love,
God.

(over →)

P.S.
Always
remember:

Yea, I have loved thee
with an everlasting
love.

Jer. 31:3